Christmas

Sheet Music For Piano

60 Best Classic Christmas Hits

Table of Contents

12 Days Of Christmas 4

All I Want for Christmas Is You 6

Angels We Have Heard on High 8

Away In A Manger 10

Believe (The Polar Express) 12

Feliz Navidad 14

Frosty The Snowman 16

Grown-Up Christmas List 18

Happy Holiday 22

Happy New Year 28

Happy Xmas (War Is Over) 30

Have Yourself A Merry Little Christmas 36

I Saw Mommy Kissing Santa Claus 38

I'll Be Home For Christmas 40

It Came Upon The Midnight Clear 42

It's The Most Wonderful Time Of The Year 44

Jingle Bell Rock 48

Joy To The World 50

March from The Nutcracker 52

Mary, Did You Know? 54

O Come, All Ye Faithful 56

Pat-a-Pan 58

Rockin' Around The Christmas Tree 60

Rudolph The Red-Nosed Reindeer 62

Santa Baby 64

Santa Claus Is Coming To Town 66

The Christmas Waltz 68

The First Noel 70

What Child Is This? 72

Winter Wonderland 74

Ave Maria 76

Auld Lang Syne 79

Blue Christmas 80

Christmas Time Is Here 83

Carol Of The Bells 84

Deck The Hall (Fa La La La) 87

Gesu Bambino 88

Go, Tell It On The Mountain 95

It's Beginning To Look A Lot Like Christmas 96

God Rest Ye Merry Gentlemen 99

Jesu, Joy Of Man's Desiring 100

Good King Wenceslas 103

Mele Kalikimaka 104

Hark! The Herald Angels Sing 107

Merry Christmas Mr. Lawrence 108

I Saw Three Ships 111

My Favorite Things 112

Jingle Bells 115

O Holy Night 116

Jolly Old Saint Nicholas 119

Silver Bells 120

Let It Snow! 123

Little Drummer Boy 124

O Christmas Tree 125

O Come, O Come Emmanuel 126

O Little Town Of Bethlehem 127

Silent Night 128

Up On The Housetop 129

We Three Kings 130

We Wish You A Merry Christmas 131

GET YOUR FREE BONUS PIANO BOOK! 132

12 Days Of Christmas

On the first day of Christ-mas my true love gave to me, a partridge in a pear

tree. On the sec-ond day of Christ-mas my true love gave to me, two tur-tle doves, and a

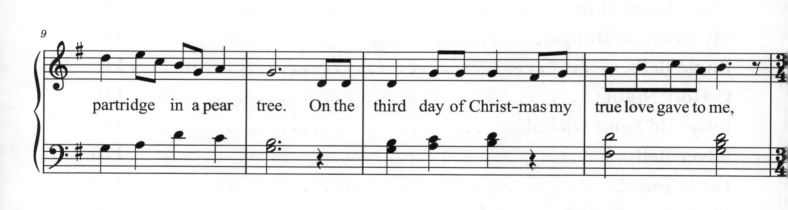

partridge in a pear tree. On the third day of Christ-mas my true love gave to me,

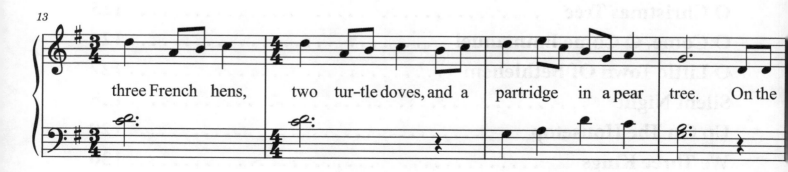

three French hens, two tur-tle doves, and a partridge in a pear tree. On the

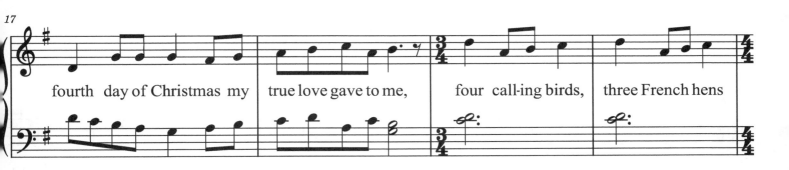

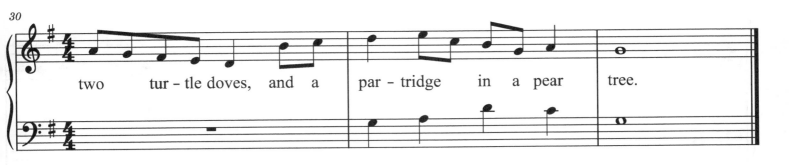

All I Want for Christmas Is You

I don't want a lot for Christ mas; there is just one thing

I need. And I don't care a bout the pre sents

un der neath the Christ mas tree. I don't need to hang

my stock ing there u pon the fi re place.

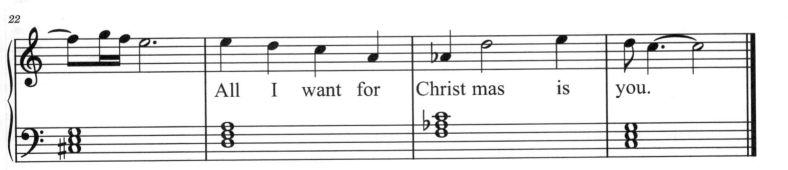

Angels We Have Heard on High

♩ = 100

1. An - gels we have heard on high, Sweet - ly sing - ing
2. Shep - herds, why this ju - bi - lee? Why your joy - ous
3. Come to Beth - le - hem and see Him whose birth the
4. See Him in a man - ger laid, Je - sus, Lord of

o'er the plains, And the moun - tains, in re - ply,
strains pro - long? What the glad - some ti - dings be
an - gels sing; Come a - dore on bend - ed knee
heav'n and earth; Ma - ry, Jo - seph, lend your aid,

Ech - o - ing their joy - ous straings. Glo
Which in - spire your heav'n - ly song?
Christ the Lord, the new - born King.
With us sing our Sav - ior's birth.

ri-a   in ex-cel-sis De-o! Glo

ri-a   in ex - cel - sis De - o!

Away In A Manger

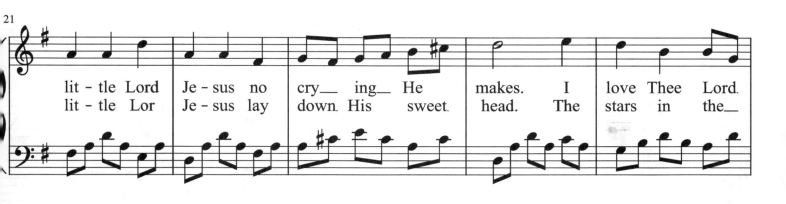

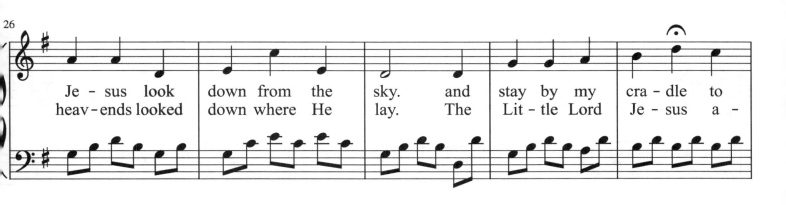

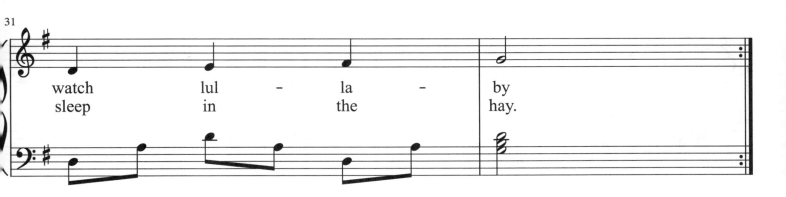

Believe (The Polar Express)

Andante

Feliz Navidad

Frosty The Snowman

Fros-ty the snowman wasa jol-ly hap-py soul, with a corn-cob pipe and a
Fros-ty the snowman is a fai-ry talethey say, he was made of snow but the

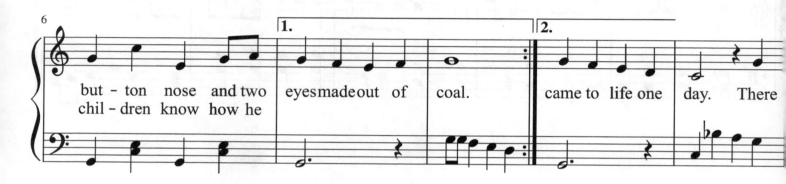

but - ton nose and two eyesmadeout of coal.
chil - dren know how he

1. eyesmadeout of coal.
2. came to life one day. There

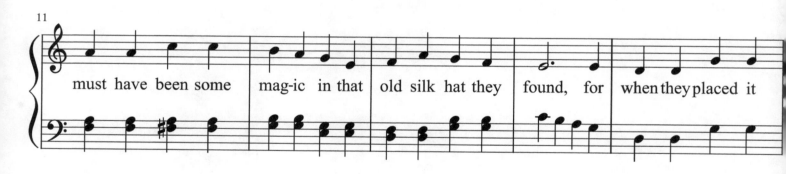

must have been some mag-ic in that old silk hat they found, for whentheyplaced it

on his head he be-gan to dance a - round! Fros-ty the snowman hadto

16

hur - ry on his way but he waved good – bye say-ing "Don't you cry, I'll be

back a - gain some day." – Thumpe - ty thump thump thum-pe - ty thump thump

look at old Fros - ty go, Thumpe - ty thump thump thumpe - ty thump thump

ov - er the hills of snow!

Grown-Up Christmas List

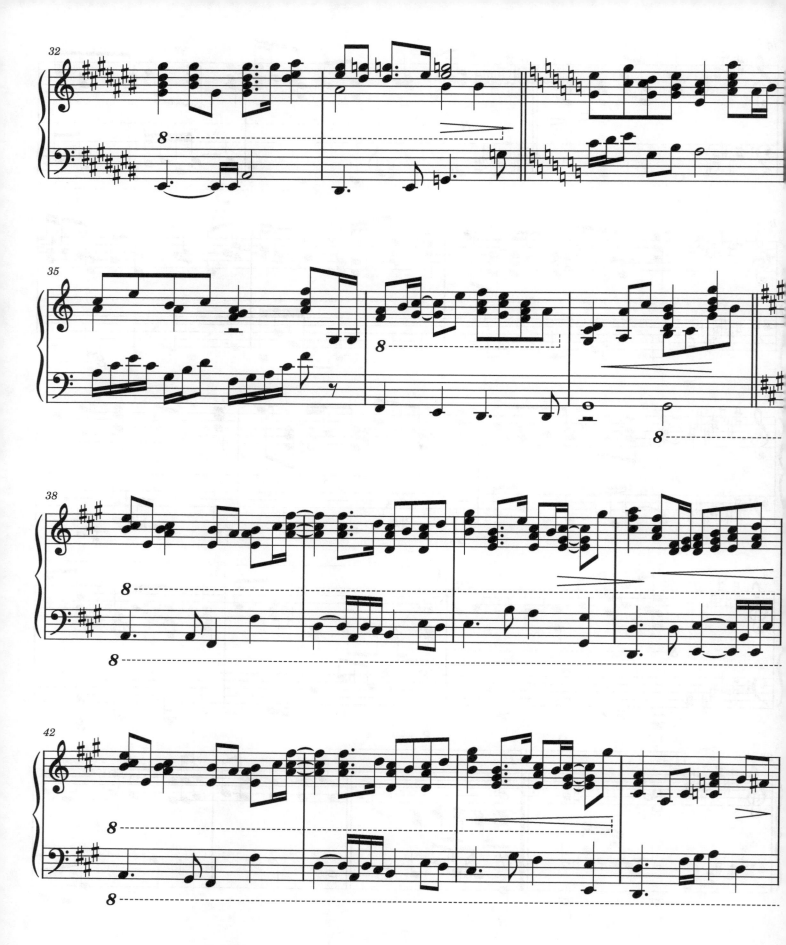

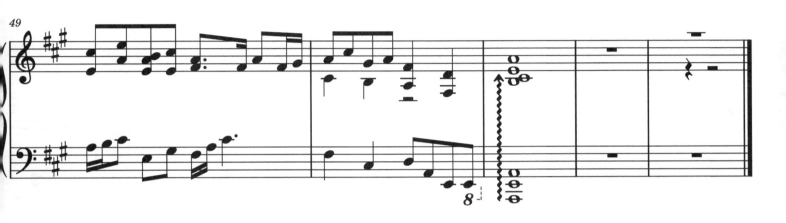

Happy Holiday

24

Happy New Year

HAPPY NEW | YEAR   HAPPY NE | YEAR   May we all | have   a
YEAR   HAPPY NE | YEAR   May we all | have   our

vi sion now and | then of the | world where ev ry | neigh bor is a
hopes our wills to | try if we | don't we might as | well lay down and

1.
f r i end   HAPPY NE

2.
d i e   You and I

Happy Xmas (War Is Over)

32

34

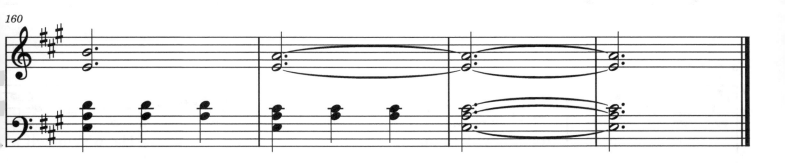

Have Yourself A Merry Little Christmas

golden days of yore; Faith-ful friends who are dear to us gather near to us once

more. Through the years we all will be togeth-er If the fates al - low.

Hang a shin-ing star up-on the high-est bough___ And have yourself a

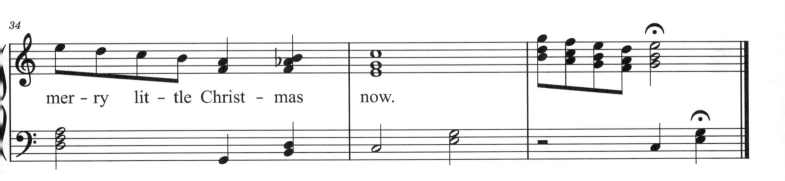

mer - ry lit - tle Christ - mas now.

I Saw Mommy Kissing Santa Claus

Moderately

mf I saw Mom-my kiss-ing San - ta Claus Un - der-neath the

mis - tle - toe last night. She did - n't see me creep Down the

stairs to have a peep; She thought that I was tucked up in my bedroom fast a -

sleep. Then I saw Mommy tick-le San - ta Claus Un-derneath his

beard so snow-y white;___ Oh, what a laugh it would have been if

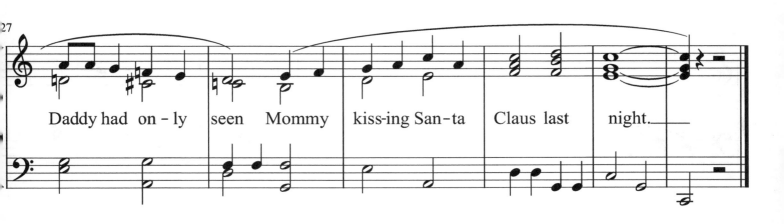

Daddy had on-ly seen Mommy kiss-ing San-ta Claus last night.___

I'll Be Home For Christmas

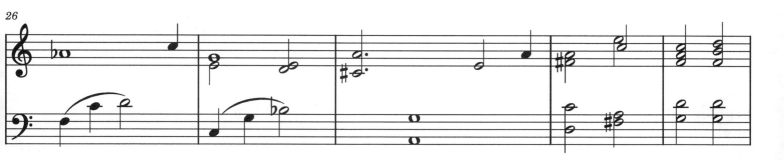

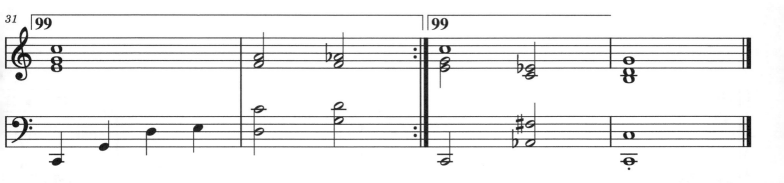

It Came Upon The Midnight Clear

It Came up-on— the mid-night clear, that glo-ri-ous

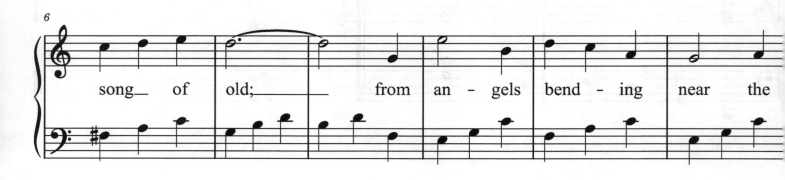

song— of old;——— from an-gels bend-ing near the

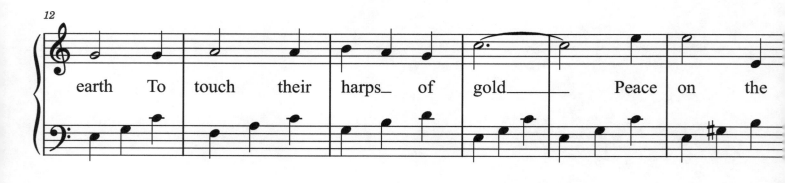

earth To touch their harps— of gold——— Peace on the

earth— good will to men, From heav-en's all gra— cious

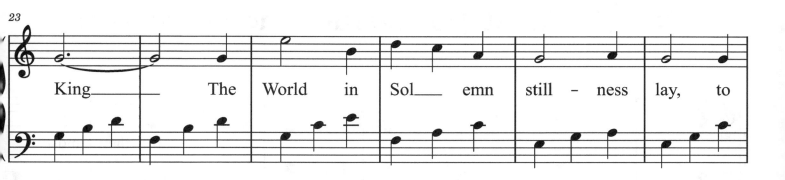

King_____ The World in Sol___ emn still - ness lay, to

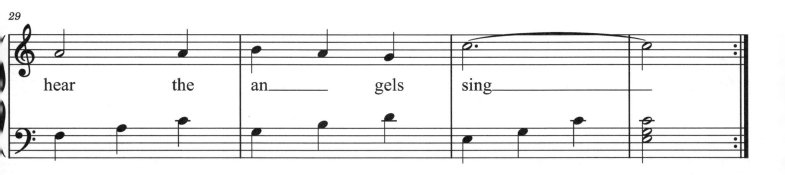

hear the an_____ gels sing_____

It's The Most Wonderful Time Of The Year

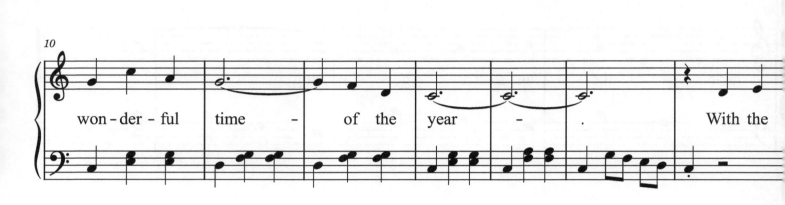

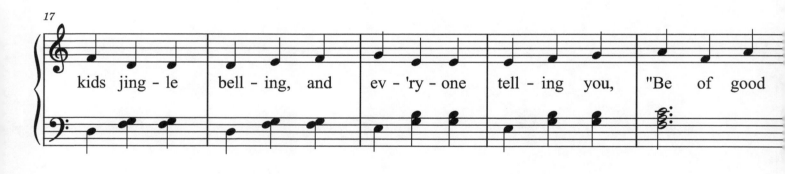

out in the snow. And there'll be scar - y ghost sto - ries and tales of the glo - ries of Christ - mas-es long long a - go.

It's the most won - der - ful time - of the year. - There'll be much mis - tle - toe - ing and hearts will be glow - ing, when loved ones are near, It's the most

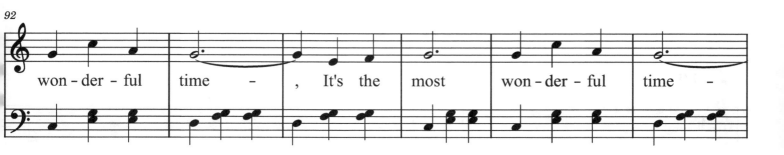

won - der - ful time   -   , It's the most   won - der - ful time   -

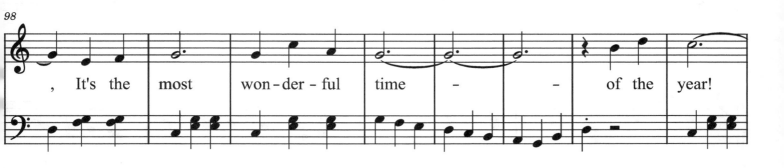

, It's the most   won - der - ful time   -   -   of the year!

Jingle Bell Rock

Jingle bell, jing-le bell, jin-gle bell rock,

Jin-gle bell swing and jin-gle bells ring. Snowin' and blowin' up bushels of fun;

now the jin-gle hop has be – gun. Jin-gle bell, jing-le bell, jin-gle bell rock,

Jin-gle bell swing and jingle bells ring. Danc-in and pranc-in in Jin-gle Bell Square,

in the frosty air. What a bright time, it's the right time to rock the night a-way.

Jin-gle bell time_ is a swell time_ to go rid-in' in a one horse sleigh._

Jin-gle bell, jingle bell, jin-gle bell rock, Jingle a-round the clock. Mix and min-gle in a

jingl-in' beat, that's the jingle bell that's the jingle bell that's the jin-gle bell

rock!

Joy To The World

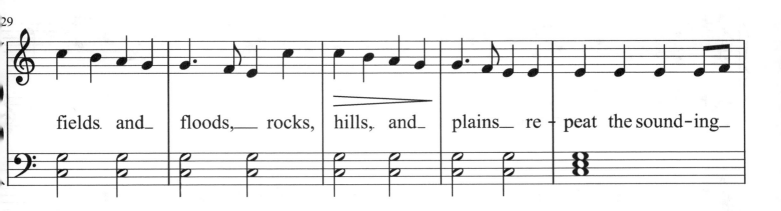

March from The Nutcracker

Mary, Did You Know?

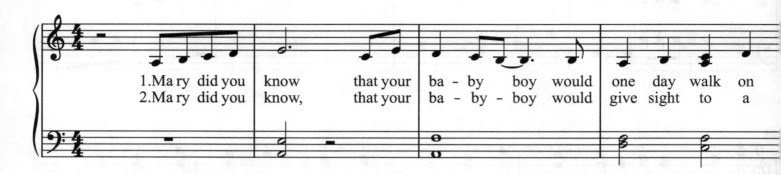

1. Ma ry did you know that your ba - by boy would one day walk on
2. Ma ry did you know, that your ba - by - boy would give sight to a

wa - ter? Ma - ry did you know that your ba - by - boy would save our sons and
blind man? Ma - ry did you know that your ba - by - boy will calm the storm with

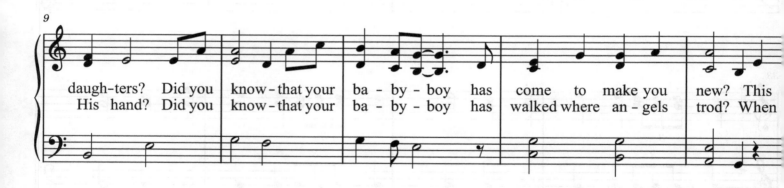

daugh-ters? Did you know - that your ba - by - boy has come to make you new? This
His hand? Did you know - that your ba - by - boy has walked where an - gels trod? When

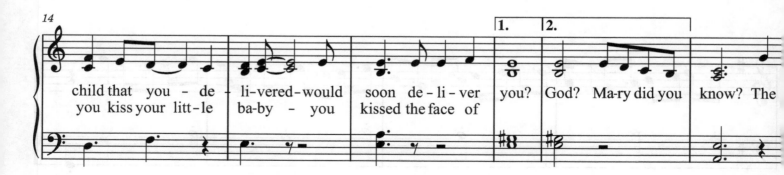

child that you - de - li-vered - would soon de - li - ver you?
you kiss your litt - le ba-by - you kissed the face of

1. you? **2.** God? Ma-ry did you know? The

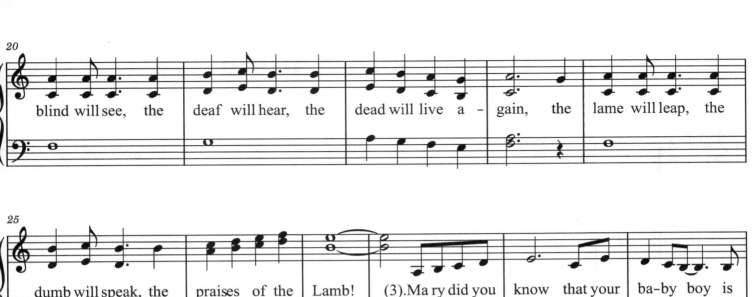

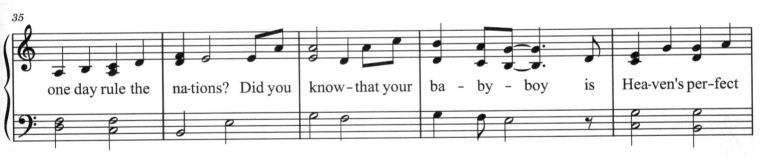

O Come, All Ye Faithful

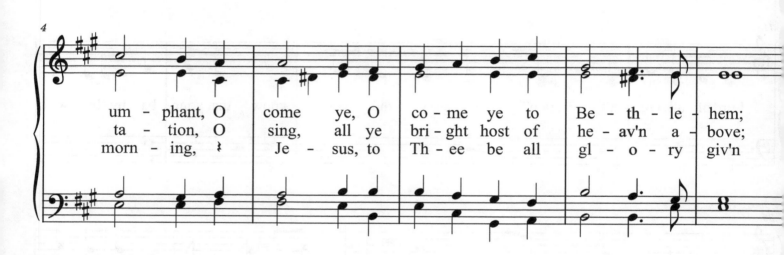

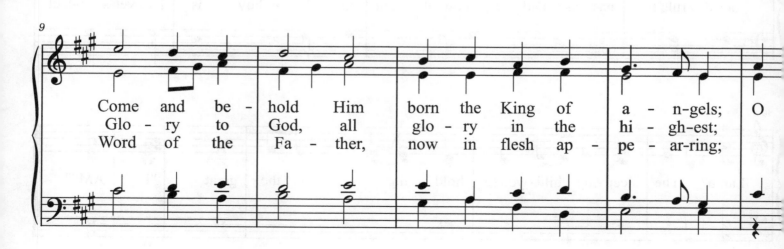

come, let us a - dore Him, O come, let us a - dore Him O

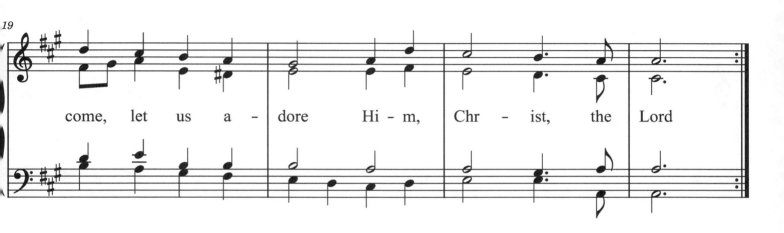

come, let us a - dore Hi - m, Chr - ist, the Lord

Pat-a-Pan

1.Wil-lie, take your lit - tle
men of old - en

1.Come, take your
2.When men of

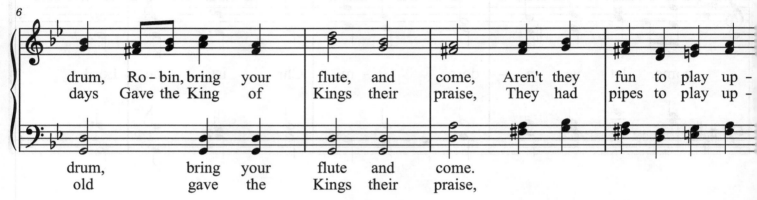

drum, Ro - bin, bring your flute, and come, Aren't they fun to play up -
days Gave the King of Kings their praise, They had pipes to play up -

drum, bring your flute and come.
old gave the Kings their praise,

on? Tu -re-lu-re - lu, pat-a-pan-a - pan; When you play you fife and
on Tu -re-lu-re - lu, pat-a-pan-a - pan; And al - so the drums they'd

drum, How can an - y - one be glum? 2.When the
play, Full of joy, on Christ - mas Day. 3.God and

man to-day be -

3.God and man

come close-ly joined as flute and drum, Let the joy-ous tune play on! Tu-re-lu-re-

are close as flute and drum,

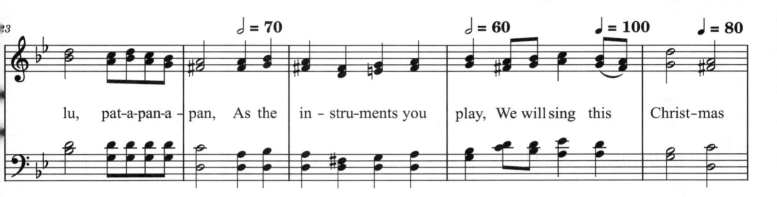

♩ = 70   ♩ = 60   ♪ = 100   ♩ = 80

lu, pat-a-pan-a - pan, As the in - stru-ments you play, We will sing this Christ-mas

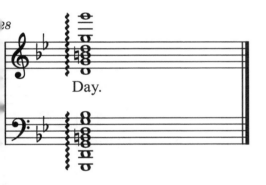

Day.

Rockin' Around The Christmas Tree

Rock in' a round the Christ mas tree at the Christ mas par ty hop.

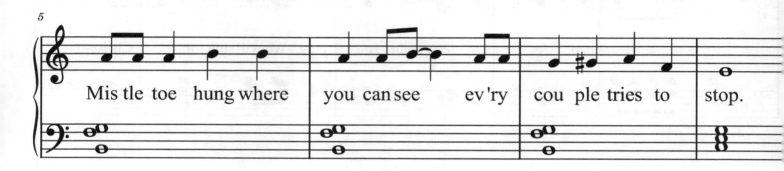

Mis tle toe hung where you can see ev'ry cou ple tries to stop.

Rock in' a round the Christ mas tree let the Christ mas spir it ring.

La ter we'll have some pump kin pie and we'll do some car ol ing.

You will get a sen ti men tal feel ing when you hear voic es sing ing

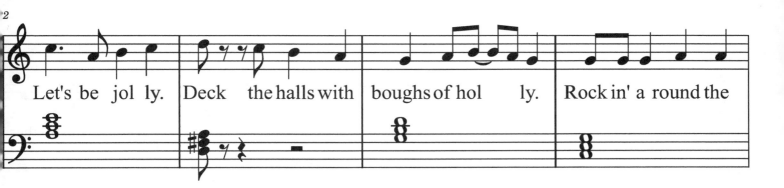

Let's be jol ly. Deck the halls with boughs of hol ly. Rock in' a round the

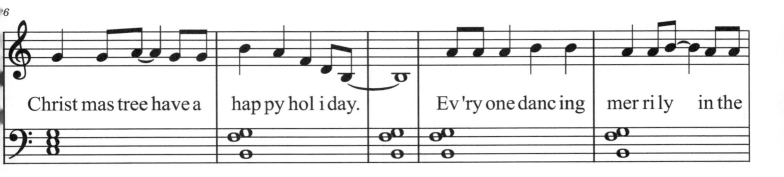

Christ mas tree have a hap py hol i day. Ev 'ry one danc ing mer ri ly in the

1. new old fash ioned way. **2.** new old fash ioned way.

Rudolph The Red-Nosed Reindeer

Ru-dolph the red - nosed reindeer Had a ve-ry shi - ny nose,

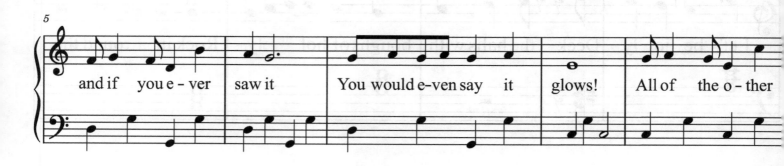

and if you e - ver saw it You would e-ven say it glows! All of the o - ther

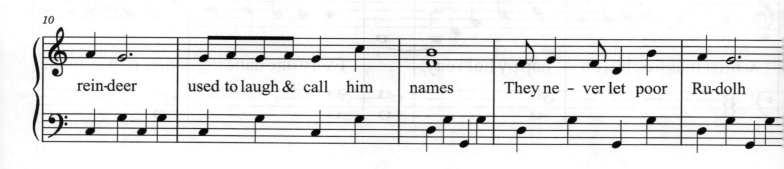

rein-deer used to laugh & call him names They ne - ver let poor Ru-dolh

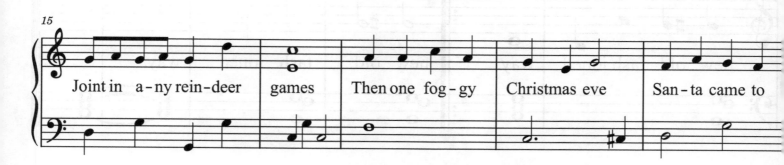

Joint in a-ny rein-deer games Then one fog-gy Christmas eve San - ta came to

Santa Baby

Santa Claus Is Coming To Town

The Christmas Waltz

The First Noel

♩ = 90

The_ first_____ No - el, The_ an - gels did say, Was to

cer - tain poor shep-herds in fields as they lay; In_ fields_____ where

they lay_ keep-ing their sheep, On a cold win-ter's night_ that

was__ so deep. No_ el_____ No - el, No_ el_____ No_

el_____ Born is the King__ of Is____ ra - el.

They looked up, and saw a star,
Shining in the East beyond them far;
And to the earth it gave great light,
And so it continued day and night.

Chorus

This star drew nigh to the north west,
O'er Bethlehem it took its rest,
And there it did both stop and stay,
Right o'er the place where Jesus lay.
Chorus

What Child Is This?

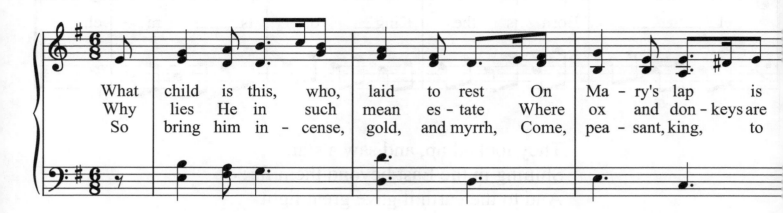

What child is this, who, laid to rest On Ma - ry's lap is
Why lies He in such mean es - tate Where ox and don - keys are
So bring him in - cense, gold, and myrrh, Come, pea - sant, king, to

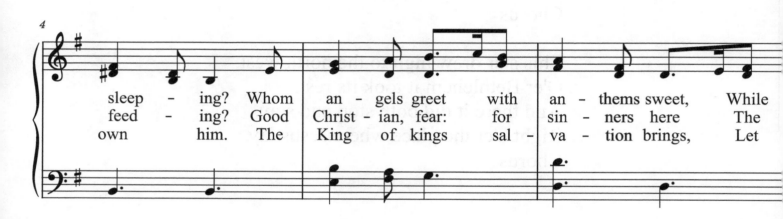

sleep - ing? Whom an - gels greet with an - thems sweet, While
feed - ing? Good Christ - ian, fear: for sin - ners here The
own him. The King of kings sal - va - tion brings, Let

shep - herds watch are keep - ing? This, this is Christ the King, Whom
Si - lent Word is plead - ing. Nails, spears shall pierce him through the
lo - ving hearts en - throne Him. Raise, raise a song on high The

Shep-herds guard and an-gels sing: Haste, haste to bring Him laud, The
cross he bore for me, for you. Hail, hail the Word made flesh, The
vir - gin sings her lul - la - by Joy, joy for Christ is born, The

babe, the son of Ma - ry.
babe, the son of Ma - ry.
babe, the son of Ma - ry.

Winter Wonderland

Ave Maria

Auld Lang Syne

♩ = 60

Should auld acquain-tance be for-got, And nev - er bro't to
here's a hand, my trust - y frien', and gie's a hand o'

mind? Should auld acquain-tance be for-got, And days of auld lang
thine? We'll tak' a cup o' kind - ness yet, For auld lang

syne? For auld lang syne, my dear, For auld lang syne; We'll
syne?

tak' a cup of kind - ness yet, For auld lang syne. And syne.

Blue Christmas

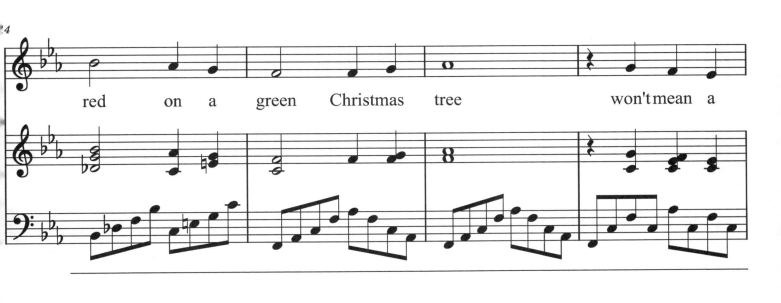

red on a green Christmas tree won't mean a

thing if you're not here with me I'll have a blue

Christ-mas that's cer-tain and when that blue

heart-ache starts hurt-ing you'll be do - ing al -

right with your Christ - mas of white but I'll have a

blue, blue Christ - mas...

Christmas Time Is Here

Carol Of The Bells

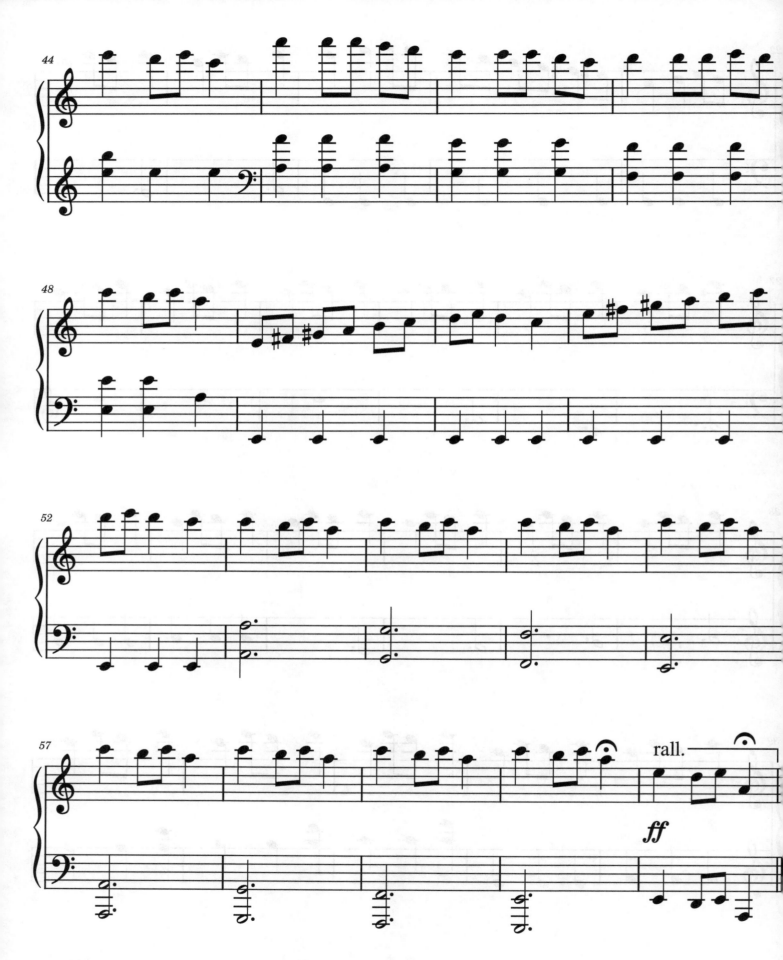

Deck The Hall (Fa La La La La)

Gesù Bambino

an gels sang - the shep – herds sang, The grate ful earth re joiced

And at His bless – ed birth the stars Their ex – ul ta – tion

voiced – – – O come let us a –

dore him O come let us a – dore him – O

come let us a – dore Him Christ – the

Lord – – – – – – A

gain the heart with rap ture glows To greet the ho ly night That

gave the world its Christ-mas Rose, Its King - of Love and light – Let

Ev' - ry voice - a - claim His name, The grate - ful cho - rus swell –

From par-a-dise to earth he came That we with Him might dwell - - O come let us a dore him O come let us a-dore Him O come let us a

dore him Christ - the lord - -

- - - Ah - - - Ve

ni - te a - do - re - mus Ah - - - ad-o

re - mus Do - minum   Ve - ni - te - ve - ni - te -

- ve - ni - te a - do - re - mus   Ah - ah - do -

re - mus - Do - mi - num

Go, Tell It On The Mountain

It's Beginning To Look A Lot Like Christmas

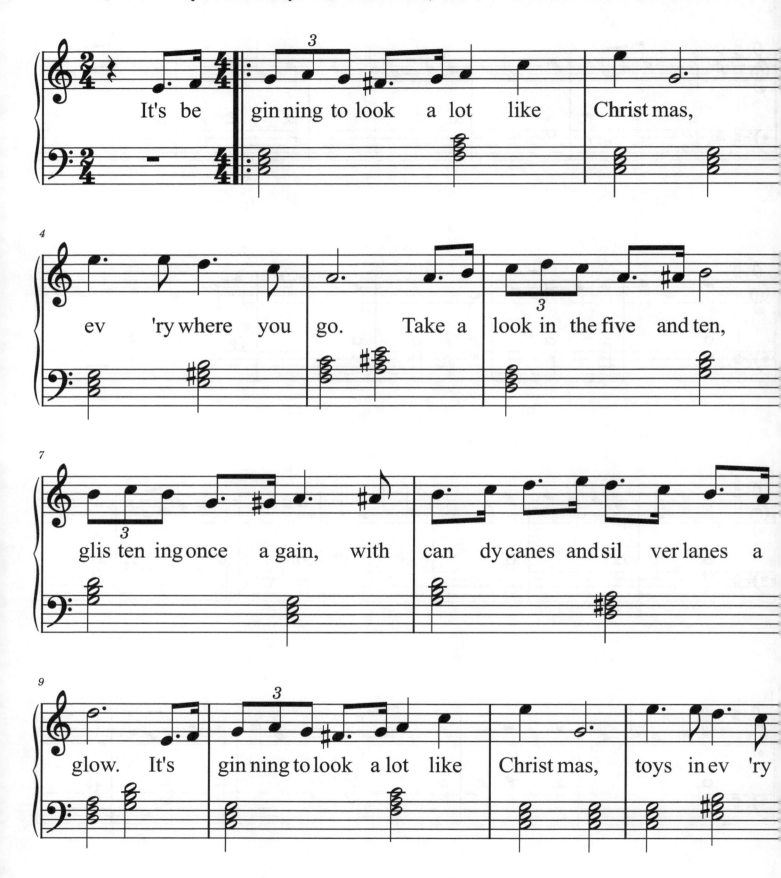

It's be- gin-ning to look a lot like Christ-mas, ev- 'ry-where you go. Take a look in the five and ten, glis-ten-ing once a-gain, with can-dy canes and sil-ver lanes a glow. It's be-gin-ning to look a lot like Christ-mas, toys in ev-'ry

store.   But   the   pret   ti   est sight   to see   is   the

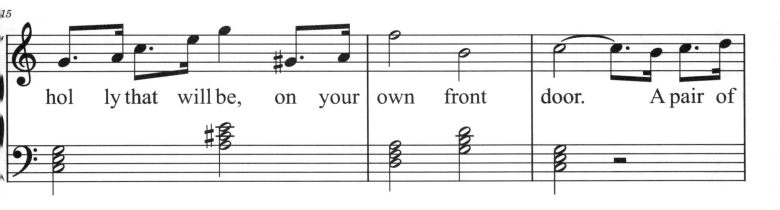

hol   ly that will be,   on   your   own   front   door.   A pair of

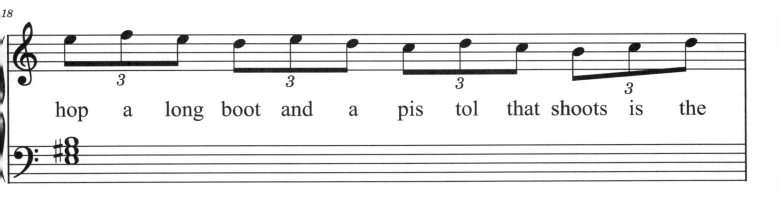

hop   a   long boot and   a   pis   tol   that shoots   is   the

wish   of   Bar   ney   and   Ben.

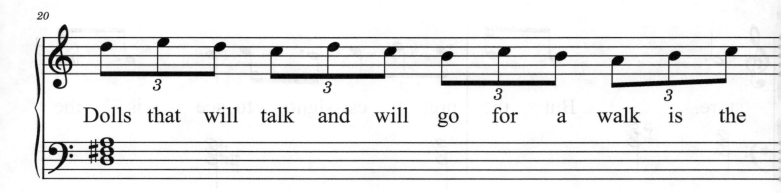

Dolls that will talk and will go for a walk is the

hope of Jan ice and Jen. And Mom and Dad can hard ly wait for

school to start a gain. It's be pret ti est sight to see is the

hol ly that will be, on your own front door.

God Rest Ye Merry Gentlemen

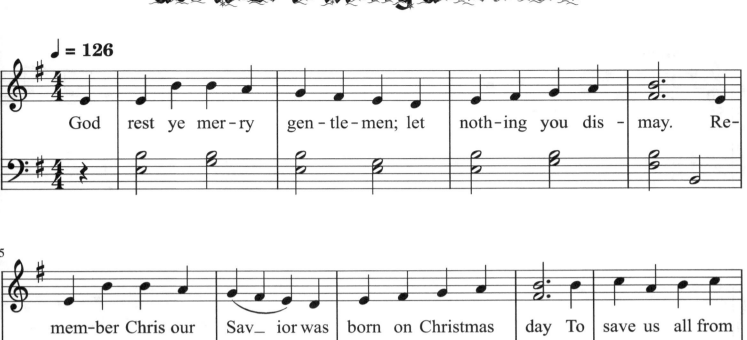

Jesu, Joy Of Man's Desiring

Good King Wenceslas

Good King Wen - ces - las looked out on the Feast of Ste - phen,

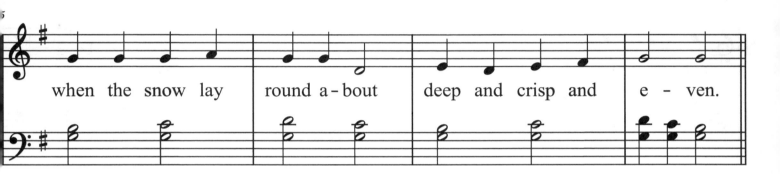

when the snow lay round a - bout deep and crisp and e - ven.

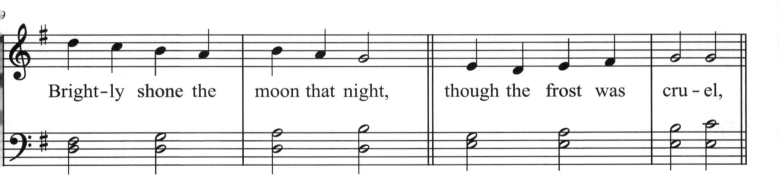

Bright-ly shone the moon that night, though the frost was cru - el,

when a poor man came in sight gath-'ring win-ter's fu - el.

Mele Kalikimaka

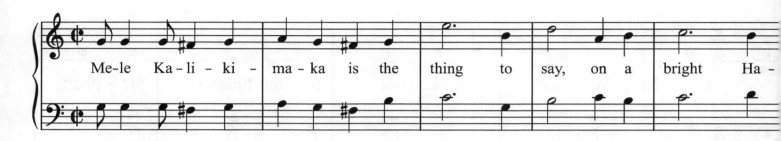

Me-le Ka-li-ki-ma-ka is the thing to say, on a bright Ha-

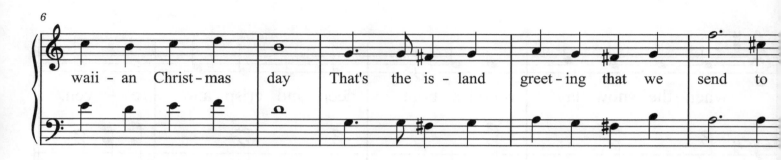

waii-an Christ-mas day That's the is-land greet-ing that we send to

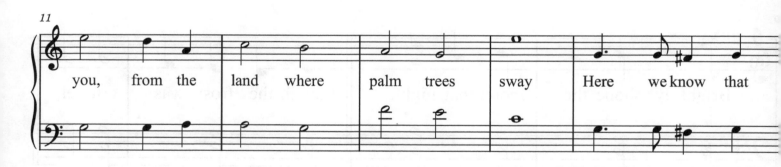

you, from the land where palm trees sway Here we know that

Christ-mas will be green and bright, the sun to shine by day and all the

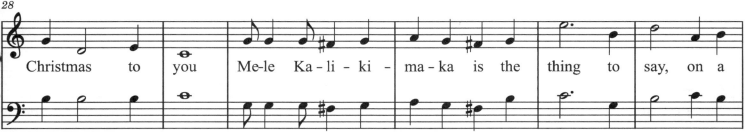

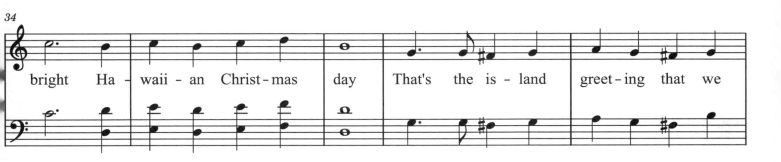

stars at night Me-le Ka - li - ki - ma - ka is Ha - wa - ii's way to say Me-rry

Christ-mas a ve-ry Me-rry Christ-mas a very very merry - merry

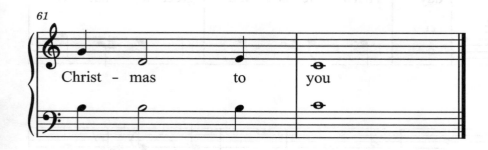

Christ - mas to you

Hark! The Herald Angels Sing

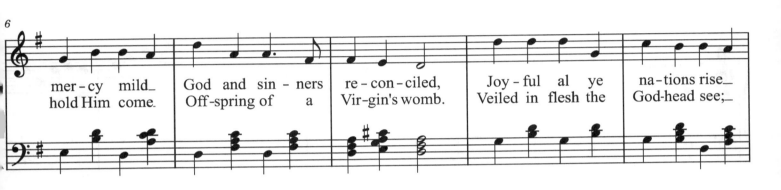

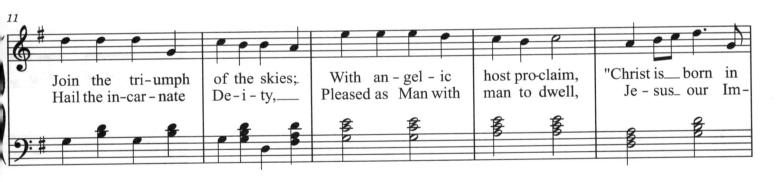

Merry Christmas Mr. Lawrence

I Saw Three Ships

I saw three ships come sail-ing in, On Christ-mas day, on Christmas day. I

saw three ships come sail-ing in, On Christ-mas day in the morn-ing

And what was in those ships all three,
On Christmas day, on Christmas day?
And what was in those ships all three,
On Christmas day in the morning?

Our saviour Christ and his lady,
On Christmas day, on Christmas day.
Our saviour Christ and his lady,
On Christmas day in the morning.

Pray whither sailed those ships all three,
On Christmas day, on Christmas day?
Pray whither sailed those ships all three,
On Christmas day in the morning?

Oh, they sailed to Bethlehem,
On Christmas day, on Christmas day.
Oh, they sailed to Bethlehem,
On Christmas day in the morning.

And all the bells on earth shall ring,
On Christmas day, on Christmas day.
And all the bells on earth shall ring,
On Christmas day in the morning.

And all the angels in heaven shall sing,
On Christmas day, on Christmas day.
And all the angels in heaven shall sing,
On Christmas day in the morning.

And all the souls on earth shall sing,
On Christmas day, on Christmas day.
And all the souls on earth shall sing,
On Christmas day in the morning.

Then let us all rejoice amain,
On Christmas day, on Christmas day.
Then let us all rejoice amain,
On Christmas day in the morning.

My Favorite Things

♩ = 145

1.Rain - drops on
2.Cream col - ored

a tempo

rit.

ros - es and whisk - ers on kit - tens, bright cop - per
pon - ies and crisp ap - ple stru - dels, door - bells and

ket - tles and warm wool - en mit - tens, brown pa - per
sleigh - bells and schnitz - el with noo - dles, wild geese that

pack ag - es tied up with strings, these are a
fly with the moon on their wings these are a

few of my fa - vor - ite things.
few of my fa - vor - ite things.

3.Girls - in white dress - es with blue sat - in sash - es, snow flakes that stay on my nose and eye lash - es sil - ver white win - ters that melt in to springs these are a

Jingle Bells

O Holy Night

♩ = 120

1. O Ho - ly Night! The stars are bright - ly shi - ning, It is the
2. Led by the light of faith se - rene - ly beam - ing, With glow - ing
3. Tru - ly He taught us love for one a - noth - er, His law is

night of our dear Sav - iour's birth_____ Long lay the world in
hearts by His cra - del we stand._____ O - ver the world a
love and His gos - pel is peace._____ Chains He shall break, the

sin and er - ror pin - ning. Till He ap - peared and the soul felt it's
star is sweet - ly gleam - ing, Now come the wise - men from O - ri - ent
slave is our broth - er, And in His name all op - pres - sion shall cease.

worth._____ A thrill of hope the wea - ry world re - joi - ces, For yon - der
land._____ The King of kings lay thus in low - ly man - ger; In all our
_____ Sweet hymns of joy in grate - ful chor - us raise we, With all our

breaks a new and glor - ious morn. Fall_____ on your knees!____ Oh, hear____
tri - als born to be our friend. He_____ knows our need,_____ our weak -
hearts we praise His ho - ly name. Christ____ is the Lord! Oh praise____

___ the an - gel voi - ces! O night_____ di - vine,____ O__ night____
- ness is no strang - er! Be - hold_____your King!____ Be - fore____
___ His name for - ev - er! His pow'r_____ and glo - ry__ ev -

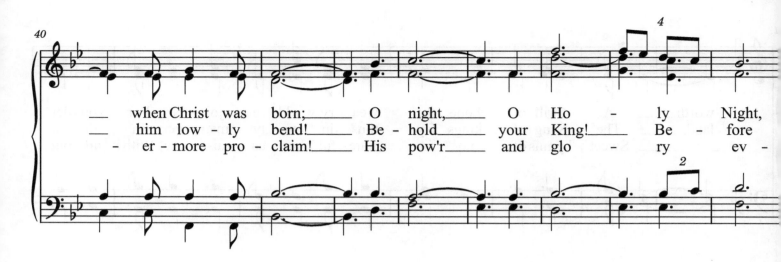

when Christ was born;____ O night,____ O Ho — ly Night,
him low - ly bend!____ Be - hold____ your King!____ Be - fore
-er-more pro - claim!____ His pow'r____ and glo — ry ev -

O night di — vine!____
Him low - ly bend!
er — more pro - claim!

Jolly Old Saint Nicholas

♩ = 120

Jol – ly old Saint Ni-cho-las, Lean your ear this way! Don't you tell a

sin-gle soul What I'm goin to say. Christ-mas Eve is coming soon;

Now you dear old man, Whis-per what you'll bring to me. Tell me if you

can.

Silver Bells

Moderato

Let It Snow!

Oh the weather out-side is fright-ful, and the fire is so de - lightful and

since we've no place to go, let it snow, let it snow, let it snow! It

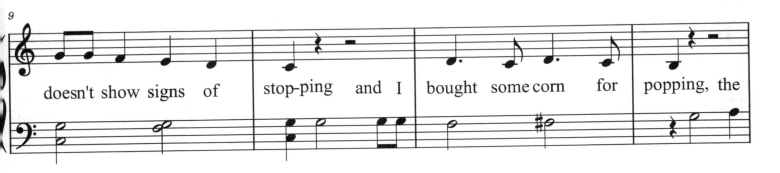

doesn't show signs of stop-ping and I bought some corn for popping, the

lights are turned way down low, let it snow, let it snow, let it snow!

Little Drummer Boy

O Christmas Tree

O Come, O Come Emmanuel

O Little Town Of Bethlehem

Silent Night

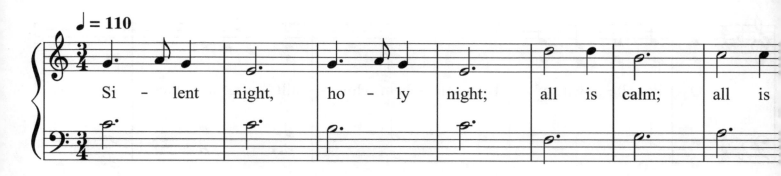

Up On The Housetop

We Three Kings

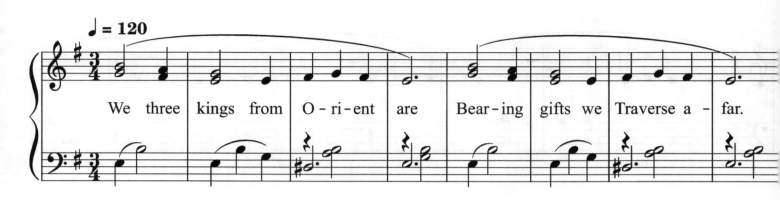

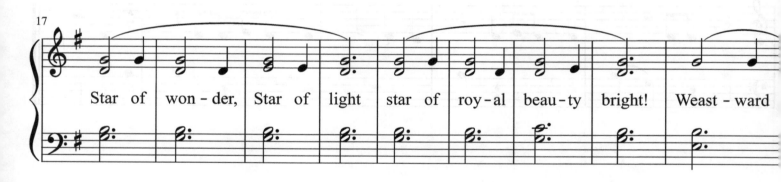

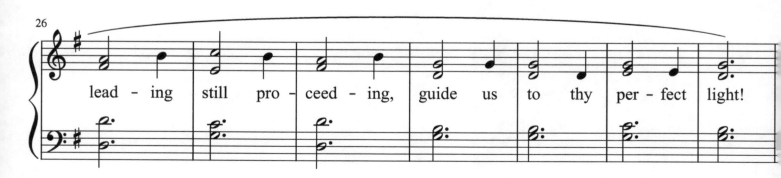

We Wish You A Merry Christmas

GET YOUR FREE BONUS PIANO BOOK!

Your Opinion Matters! Help Us Shape the Future of Piano Music

Dear Valued Customer,

We hope this message finds you well and that your musical journey continues to be a harmonious and fulfilling one. We wanted to reach out to you today to express our heartfelt gratitude for choosing our piano book «CHRISTMAS SHEET MUSIC FOR PIANO», to be your companion on this melodious adventure.

As creators and musicians ourselves, we understand the pivotal role that feedback plays in refining and enhancing our craft. Your insights and opinions are invaluable to us, and we believe they have the power to shape the future of piano music. That's why we kindly request you to take a few moments out of your day to leave a review for «CHRISTMAS SHEET MUSIC FOR PIANO».

Your review will not only help us understand what aspects of the book resonated with you the most but also guide us in making improvements to provide an even more enriching experience for aspiring pianists like yourself. By sharing your thoughts, you become an integral part of our creative process, and your contribution will be felt by countless others who embark on this musical journey.

Whether you found the exercises particularly helpful, the sheet music beautifully arranged, or the accompanying explanations insightful, your honest review will help fellow musicians make informed decisions. Your words could be the encouragement someone else needs to dive into the world of piano music and unlock their artistic potential.

Leaving a review is easy:
* Just scan QR Code with your phone and leave a good review if you like the book.

Thank you once again for choosing our book, and we eagerly await your insights. Together, we can create a harmonious and inspiring environment for every pianist to thrive.

May your music continue to resonate with passion and grace!

Warm regards,

Henry White

Made in United States
Troutdale, OR
11/16/2023

14646838R00077